YONANAS

THE ULTIMATE GUIDE FOR DELICIOUS ICE CREAM RECIPES

professional before attempting any techniques outlined in this book.

Introduction

Healthy desserts are easier to make than you think. This is a frozen dessert that is as healthy for you as it is delicious. You will find that it is made from things that you may already have in your kitchen.

The dessert is called 'Yonanas'. It is made with frozen bananas that are frozen and placed in a food processor. They are processed until they have the consistency of soft-serve ice cream. The Banana soft serve is then mixed with olive oil, cinnamon, honey, and vanilla. After this, the mixture is put in a pan and freeze in the freezer for about 24 - 36 hours. In the last hour of freezing the Yonanas is evenly sliced and then carefully arranged on a plate in a circular pattern. They are finished with a drizzle of honey.

These desserts can be eaten almost like you would eat soft serve ice cream. You can take a spoon and eat it, or you could make a sundae. They are simple enough that a child could make them, so they could even make them for their family if they wanted to.

The benefits of the Yonanas are that it contains no added sugar or artificial sweeteners.

With the market saturated with blenders and ice cream makers, the Yonanas was a simple recipe to perfect. The Yonanas frozen desserts are gluten-free and vegan. They also contain no cholesterol. The Yonanas includes a large amount of potassium. It also is a good source of vitamin C and magnesium. Yonanas is an excellent source of fiber.

The Yonanas may be kept frozen for long periods. They are a fun dessert to eat, and they are nutritious.

Pros & Cons

We consider the Yonanas Healthy Dessert Maker® to be a fantastic choice for your household frozen dessert appliance. We want you to weigh all your options. Make informed decisions. Here are some Pros and Cons of the machine.

Pros

Healthy-Frozen fruits make this a healthy option. Less sugar and dairy-free, if you want.

You choose your ingredients. You control what goes into the machine. There are so many options, both healthy and not so healthy. The elements and combinations are endless.

Super easy to use-Fill the chute, press down on the plastic plunger to send ingredients through the tube, and enjoy. It is that easy. 1-2-3.

Multipurpose-Dishwasher safe- Even though you have to take apart and rinse the individual pieces, you can quickly pop them into the dishwasher.

The lightweight-The machine itself is super lightweight and very easy to move around. You can take it to a friend's house or an event so quickly.

It's fun to experiment-This is the number one reason to purchase the Yonanas Healthy Dessert Maker. It's fun. The possibilities are endless. You can toss in whatever sweet treats you have lying around your home and have an instant creamy dessert.

Cons

Noisy- While this machine is not much more robust than a blender, many users have mentioned that it is deafening. The Yonanas Elite Frozen Healthy Dessert Maker® is said to be a bit quieter.

Not a breeze to clean-Dishwasher safe doesn't mean pop the whole thing into the dishwasher. Frozen fruits can be tricky and get sticky if not rinsed right away. Unscrewing the parts and rinsing them under warm water or soaking them for a while can help cut back on the cleaning issues many users complain about.

Letting the fruit thaw-The guide book suggests letting the frozen fruit sit on the counter for about 5 - 10 minutes. But waiting that extra time can be hard to do. When you want ice cream, you want it right then. But if the fruit doesn't thaw the texture is very gritty and not as creamy as it should be. So, pause for the cause and wait that extra few minutes.

Challenging to make large quantities-It could take a while if you're trying to feed a bunch of people, and by the time you've popped out 4 bowls the first bowl is well on its way to fully melt.

Many leftovers caught inside the machine-This can be wasteful, not to mention the number of ingredients it can take to create one actual serving.

Texture Guide

Not all frozen treats are created equal. Different desserts are made with different ingredients, thus yielding different textures and flavors. Here is a cheat sheet to help you decide which one suits you best.

- **Ice Cream**

Cool and creamy, this dessert is usually made with milk. It also typically contains sugar or corn syrup for a very sweet flavor.

- **Sorbet**

If the fruit is your thing then sorbet should be your go-to frozen treat. The texture is rough and somewhat icy, as sorbet is almost always dairy-free. Flavors are refreshing and zestier tasting than creamy.

- **Sherbet**

Not to get confused with sorbet, Sherbet typically contains dairy. The taste is similar to sorbet in that it is refreshing and fruity, but sherbet will have a creamier texture and flavor because of the dairy content. Keep in mind that nondairy milk will yield equally smooth results, so don't rule sherbet out completely if you're going for a dairy-free dessert.

- **Popsicle**

Popsicles aren't always frozen, icy treats, some can have a fudgy or creamy texture. Most Popsicles are frozen using Popsicle trays with sticks, but Popsicle bites are becoming a new trend. Using ice cube trays, with no sticks, Popsicle recipes can be transformed into bite-sized treats in fun shapes. The bites are also easier to transport in baggies or containers.

- **Gelato**

Rich. Decadent. Elegant. All words that accurately describe gelato. It is almost always higher in sugar and will have a softer texture as it does not freeze completely.

- **Frozen Yogurt**

Made with Yogurt. Whether it is Greek yogurt, regular yogurt, low-fat, or coconut yogurt you can bet on yogurt being in your...well.... frozen yogurt. While sugar is sometimes added, this frozen treat has a little bit of a bite or hint of sour to it because yogurt is the main ingredient. Fruit and chocolate complement almost any fro-you flavor.

Pantry Stocking Guide

The possibilities with your Yonanas Healthy Dessert Maker® are virtually endless. The good news is that many recipes use the same, or similar, ingredients. You can always make ahead and freeze your treats.

Since many of these ingredients come frozen or are non-perishable, it makes sense to purchase them in bulk.

List of the most mentioned ingredients in this book. Use it as a guide for your shopping list.

- **Sugar:** you can always use natural sweeteners, but if you choose to use sugar try to find a quick dissolve, superfine sugar. Regular sugar can also be run through a food processor to make it finer. It makes for a less grainy texture.
- **Honey, agave nectar, or stevia:** natural sweeteners are a go-to for healthy desserts. The taste isn't changed that much and they are

low-glycemic. The honey and nectar can also create a nice binding agent for some recipes.

- **Frozen bananas:** buy them in bulk, like they are going out of style. Most recipes will call for a banana or 2. You can buy pre-sliced frozen bananas in very large quantities.
- **Cheetah spotted bananas:** stock up on fresh bananas too. The cheetah spotted ones are the sweetest. Be sure they are "cheetah spotted" and not completely brown. Peel and slice into 1/4 inch thick pieces. Store in a freezer bag or container for future use.
- **Frozen fruits:** every recipe is going to call for some kind of frozen fruit. The possibilities are limitless, so buy any frozen fruit you like. Strawberries, blueberries, raspberries, blackberries, cherries, melons, peaches, pineapples, and mangos are some of the most popular.
- **Fresh fruits:** buy and freeze your favorites. Pineapples, mangos, peaches, kiwi, and grapes are some of the popular fruits that are difficult to find already frozen. Just buy the fruit fresh, slice it into 1/4 inch thick pieces and freeze into freezer bags or containers until you're ready to use them.
- **Peanut butter:** peanut butter can be pretty awesome in frozen treats. Stock up if that's your thing.
- **Nutella:** everyone's hazelnut favorite.
- **Cocoa powder:** sweetened or unsweetened, cocoa powder is found in chocolate recipes. A lot goes a long way, plus you can usually find it in an easily sealable container.

- **Milk:** chose your flavor. Many healthy options are available like almond, soy, and coconut milk, and come in different flavors. The boxed milk can be found on the sale and not refrigerated. You can store these in your pantry until you are ready to use them.
- **Canned coconut milk:** not to be confused with boxed or refrigerated coconut milk. Canned coconut milk separates. The top part is usually a thick layer of what is referred to as "coconut cream," and the bottom part is "coconut milk." All recipes will call for the canned milk to be refrigerated. It is okay to store the can in the fridge before it has been opened.
- **Greek yogurt:** Greek yogurt has a thicker consistency than regular yogurt. This helps for a thicker dessert. Its flavor is also a little bit tarter than regular yogurt. Be sure to buy regular, vanilla, and low-fat or fat-free varieties.
- **Toasted nuts:** walnuts, pecan, cashews, peanuts. Choose whichever nuts you would like to use. Typically, a garnish.
- **Coconut flakes:** toasted coconut flakes complement many desserts.
- **Chocolate chips:** used as a garnish and also as chunks run through the machine. Regular size or minis.
- **Sprinkles:** rainbow, colored, or chocolate! Jazz up your dessert.
- **Dark chocolate:** choose bars of dark chocolate. Recipes range from 70%-85%.

- **Cookies:** pies and cakes use different cookie crumbs for the crust. Graham crackers, Oreos, and gingersnaps are some of the most popular.
- **Canola Oil:** a few tablespoons of canola oil are added to cookie crumbs to make pie crusts.
- **Eggs:** large.
- **Pie crusts:** frozen pie crusts can cut back on prep time.
- **Lemons and limes:** add a little kick. Many of the refreshing recipes will ask for lemon and lime zest or juice.
- **Extracts:** vanilla, almond, and peppermint are some of the big ones.
- **Coffee:** get your breakfast juice on. Seriously, everyone needs an excuse for eating ice cream for breakfast. So, try some coffee recipes and give yourself a reason.

Taste Hacking Guide

Let's be honest, while smoothies and blended treats can be the easiest to make, things can and do, go terribly wrong. Not everything turns out the way it should, resulting in an end product being too bitter, too thin, too thick, or even too sweet (yes, that is actually a thing). Not to worry, here are some simple fixes for your Yonanas Healthy Dessert Maker®.

1. When it's too bitter

While green veggies can be a main component of smoothies, they can also be the main contributor to that unwelcome bitter taste. But don't remove the greens! Try using baby spinach because it has a gentler flavor. Use sweeter fruits. Try pairing greens with fruits like bananas, pineapples, dates, blueberries, or strawberries. The sweet flavors will complement the bitter greens and make them not as harsh. Stevia, honey, agave nectar, and vanilla are some great natural sweeteners that will help counteract any bitterness, but be careful; a little goes a long way. If a sweet flavor wouldn't be your first choice, opt for some lemon or lime juice. The juice cuts through the bitterness and can create a refreshing cool taste. Consider adding protein powder too. Not only will it boost protein intake of course, but the powders come in fun flavors that can add a twist to any treat.

2. When it's too sweet

It happens. Every once in a while, you get a super sweet smoothie. The first fix is if you're adding sugar or other sweeteners, just don't. The smallest amount can add an explosion of flavor. Consider using low-glycemic fruits like blackberries, grapefruits, or avocados. If using milk or other additives opt for the unsweetened or sugar-free version. And of course, the end-all, be-all, fix-all is to add some lemon or lime juice and get a refreshing burst of flavor instead.

3. When it's too thick

If your smoothies come out too thick, try adding some water, milk, coffee, or juice, but be sure not to add too much. Use less frozen and fresher. Sometimes the frozen fruits can be too thick and hard and not produce enough juice to thin out the smoothie. Next time try alternating liquids and solids, putting liquids in first.

4. When it's too thin

Sometimes they come out too thin. We're going' for smoothies and frozen treats here folks, not juices! If you run into this super common issue, try using fruits with thick skins. Peaches, mangos, dates, and apricots make perfect thickeners. Bananas, avocados, and Greek yogurt are great too. Alternate the adding of liquids and solids. Add fruits and veggies first. This prevents all the liquid from pooling. Guar gum and xanthan gum are great options, especially for alcoholic treats that tend to get runny. Both are gluten-free. They function like gluten and help to bind and create volume. Just like sweeteners, a little of these additives go a long way. Try only using 1/8 of a teaspoon; otherwise, you will have another consistency issue on your hands.

5. When it's too sour

Some desserts are made to be tangy and sour, but then again too much of anything is never a good thing. Try adding more bananas or other sweeter fruits to help off put the sourness. If the recipe calls for milk or other liquids trying to add an additional tablespoon, just don't overdo it or it will get runny. When all else fails, add some sugar or natural sweeteners like honey, agave nectar, or stevia.

Ice Cream Recipes

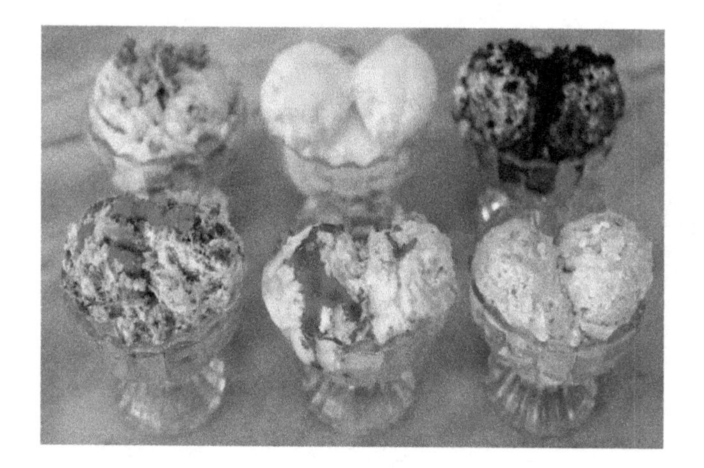

Cherry Vanilla Frozen

Preparation Time: 1 hour and 45 minutes

Cooking Time: 1 hour

Servings: 6-8

Ingredients:

- 2 cans pitted dark sweet cherries, drained
- 2 cups vanilla Greek yogurt
- 1 can evaporated milk
- 1/3 cup white sugar
- 1/2 cup half-and-half
- 1/2 cup of milk
- 1 jigger crème de cassis liqueur

Directions:

1. Squeeze cherries in a food processor until chopped. Transport to a bowl. Attach yogurt, evaporated milk, sugar, half-and-half, milk, and crème de cassis liqueur; mix well.
2. Stream into an electric mixer and mix.
3. Flow the chilled mixture into a freeze-proof container and freeze until it reaches the right mixture.

4. Transport frozen yogurt to a one- or two-quarts lidded plastic container, use plastic wrap to cover.

Nutrition:

- Calories: 165
- Protein: 138 g
- Carbs: 23 g
- Fat: 10 g
- Sugar: 8 g

Almond Delight Ice Cream Recipe

Preparation Time: 1 hour and 45 minutes

Cooking Time: 1 hour

Servings: 4

Ingredients:

- 1 1/2 cups white sugar
- 4 large eggs, beaten until light and fluffy
- 4 cups heavy whipping cream
- 2 cups of milk
- 4 teaspoons vanilla extract
- 4 teaspoons almond extract
- 1 1/4 cups sliced almonds

Directions:

1. Beat sugar into the eggs in small amounts, assuring each addition dissolves completely before introducing the next.
2. Whip cream, milk, vanilla extract, and almond extract into the egg mixture.
3. Stream into the container of an ice cream maker and freeze.

Nutrition:

- Calories: 185
- Protein: 168 g
- Carbs: 25 g
- Fat: 15 g
- Sugar: 18 g

Amaretto Ice Cream

Preparation Time: 2 hours and 45 minutes

Cooking Time: 3 hours

Servings: 4-8

Ingredients:

- 2 cups heavy whipping cream
- 1 cup half-and-half
- 3/4 cup white sugar
- 5 tablespoons amaretto liqueur
- 1 teaspoon vanilla extract

Directions:

1. Combine heavy cream, half-and-half, and sugar in a huge bowl until sugar is dissolved. Add amaretto liqueur and vanilla extract.
2. Stream milk mixture into an ice cream maker and freeze based on the manufacturer's instructions until ice cream reaches 'soft-serve' consistency. Transfer ice cream to a lidded container.
3. Freeze for about 2 hours before serving.

Nutrition:

- Calories: 185
- Protein: 168 g
- Carbs: 25 g
- Fat: 15 g
- Sugar: 18 g

Apple Pie Ice Cream

Preparation Time: 2 hours

Cooking Time: 1 hour and 30 minutes

Servings: 4-8

Ingredients:

- 8 oatmeal cookies, crushed
- 2 tablespoons melted butter, divided
- 2 large apples, peeled, cored, and sliced
- 3 tablespoons white sugar
- 1 teaspoon ground cinnamon
- 3 cups whipping cream
- 1 1/2 cups half and half
- 1 cup white sugar
- 3 large eggs
- 1/2 teaspoon vanilla extract
- 2 1/4 teaspoons ground cinnamon
- 1/4 cup toasted walnuts
- 1/4 cup caramel ice cream topping

Directions:

1. Preheat oven to 375 ^{0}F.
2. Combine the crushed cookies with melted butter, and squeeze onto a baking sheet. Bake in preheated oven for 5 minutes, then remove, allow cooling completely.
3. Dissolve the rest of the butter and whip in the apples, 3 tablespoons sugar, and 1 teaspoon cinnamon. Cook before apples have lightly browned, and the sugar has begun to caramelize about 10 minutes. Remove from the pan, and invite to cool completely.
4. Combine the cream, half and half, 1 cup of sugar, eggs, vanilla, and 2 teaspoons of cinnamon in a sizable bowl; mix to blend well. Stream into an ice cream maker and freeze

Nutrition:

- Calories: 205
- Protein: 68 g
- Carbs: 125 g
- Fat: 60 g
- Sugar: 13.9 g

Avocado Ice Cream Recipe

Preparation Time: 45 minutes

Cooking Time: 1 hour and 30 minutes

Servings: 4-8

Ingredients:

- 2 cups of water
- 1 cup white sugar
- 3 small avocados, peeled and pitted
- 1 can evaporated milk
- 1/2 cup 1% milk
- 3 tablespoons lime juice

Directions:

1. Stream the water into a saucepan, and boil; whip in sugar until dissolved. Take the syrup back again to a boil, reduce heat, and boil gently until the syrup is reduced to at least one 1 cup, about ten minutes. Remove from heat, and allow cooling.
2. Crush the avocados to your desired consistency. Combine in the evaporated milk, and lime juice. Whip in the cooled sugar syrup until completely incorporated.

3. Stream the chilled mix into an ice cream maker, and freeze. Pack the ice cream right into a lidded container, and freeze until firm, at least one hour.

Nutrition:

- Calories: 205
- Protein: 68 g
- Carbs: 125 g
- Fat: 60 g
- Sugar: 13.9 g

Japanese Red Beans Ice Cream

Preparation Time: 45 minutes

Cooking Time: 1 hour and 30 minutes

Servings: 4-8

Ingredients:

- 1 cup dry adzuki beans
- 1/3 cup white sugar
- 2 teaspoons lemon juice
- 3 1/2 cups water
- 1 cup of milk
- 1 cup heavy cream
- 4 large eggs yolks egg yolks
- 2/3 cup white sugar
- 1 teaspoon vanilla extract

Directions:

1. Combine the red beans, 1/3 cup of sugar, lemon juice, and water. Until it boils, and boil uncovered for three minutes. Decrease the heat to low, and simmer for 2 1/2 to 3 hours, or before beans are very tender.
2. Shear the bean mixture through a sieve

3. Combine the milk and cream.
4. Whip together the egg yolks and 2/3 cup of sugar in a bowl. Serve about 1/4 cup of the hot liquid into the bowl with the egg yolks, and whip until smooth.
5. Steam the yolk mixture into the pan with the cream, and cook over low heat.
6. Refrigerate until cold.
7. Once both mixtures are cold, whisk them together. Stream into an ice cream maker, and freeze.

Nutrition:

- Calories: 105
- Protein: 98 g
- Carbs: 175 g
- Fat: 67 g
- Sugar: 17 g

Banana and Peanut Butter Ice Cream

Preparation Time: 1 hour and 45 minutes

Cooking Time: 1 hour and 30 minutes

Servings: 8

Ingredients:

- 2 slightly overripe bananas cut into chunks
- 1 teaspoon confectioners' sugar
- 1 1/2 teaspoon milk
- 2 teaspoons vanilla extract
- 1 teaspoon peanut butter,

Directions:

1. Set the banana chunks on a plate; freeze until solid, about 2 hours.
2. Combine frozen bananas, confectioners' sugar, milk, and vanilla extract together in a blender add peanut butter and blend until smooth.

Nutrition:

- Calories: 155
- Protein: 95 g
- Carbs: 145 g

- Fat: 69 g
- Sugar: 19 g

Banana Ice Cream

Preparation Time: 1 hour and 45 minutes

Cooking Time: 1 hour and 30 minutes

Servings: 8

Ingredients:

- 2 cups skim milk
- 1/2 can evaporated milk
- 1/4 cup white sugar
- 1 teaspoon vanilla extract
- 2 medium bananas, mashed
- 1/2 cup golden raisins

Directions:

1. Combine together the skim milk, evaporated milk, sugar, and vanilla. Stream into an ice cream maker, and freeze based on the manufacturer's instructions.
2. When the ice cream is processed, add the bananas and raisins and let them mix in. Transport to a freezer container, and freeze overnight before serving to enhance the texture.

Nutrition:

- Calories: 155
- Protein: 95 g
- Carbs: 145 g
- Fat: 69 g
- Sugar: 19 g

Banana Mud Ice Cream

Preparation Time: 45 minutes

Cooking Time: 1 hour and 30 minutes

Servings: 4

Ingredients:

- 1 banana, sliced
- 2 tablespoons coconut milk
- 1/4 cup unsweetened cocoa powder
- 1 scoop protein powder
- 2 tablespoons peanut butter
- 2 tablespoons maple syrup
- 1 packet stevia powder

Directions:

1. Transport sliced banana into the fridge for 6 hours.
2. Mingle banana and coconut milk together in a small food processor or small blender until just smooth.
3. Attach cocoa powder, protein powder, peanut butter, maple syrup, and stevia powder; blend until smooth.

Nutrition:

- Calories: 165
- Protein: 93 g
- Carbs: 45 g
- Fat: 169 g
- Sugar: 19 g

Banana Pudding Ice Cream

Preparation Time: 45 minutes

Cooking Time: 1 hour and 30 minutes

Servings: 4-5

Ingredients:

- 1 1/2 cups half-and-half
- 1/2 cup packed light brown sugar
- 1/2 cup white sugar
- 1 pinch salt
- 2 large eggs, beaten
- 1 cup heavy whipping cream
- 1 teaspoon vanilla extract
- 2 medium very ripe bananas,
- 1/2 1 cup crushed vanilla wafers

Directions:

1. Combine brown sugar, white sugar, and salt in a saucepan cook and whisk until sugars are dissolved, about five minutes, whisk eggs into the mixture until well combined.

2. Transport egg mixture back to the pan. Cook and whisk mixture until cream mixture is thickened and coats the trunk of a spoon, 5 to 10 minutes. Detach saucepan and whisk in vanilla extract.
3. Stream cream mixture over a fine-mesh sieve and let it cool. Stir mashed bananas into cooled cream mixture.
4. Stream banana cream mixture into an ice maker and freeze.

Nutrition:

- Calories: 265
- Protein: 193 g
- Carbs: 45 g
- Fat: 169 g
- Sugar: 19 g

Sorbet Recipe

Lemon-Lime Soda Sorbet

Preparation Time: 1 hour and 45 minutes

Cooking Time: 1 hour

Servings: 6-8

Ingredients:

- 1 cup of sugar
- 1 can lemon-lime soda
- 1 1/2 cup lemon juice
- 1/2 cup lime juice

Directions:

1. Combine the sugar and soda in a small pot, and whip until the sugar is dissolved. Let it cool and unite with the lemon and lime juice. Refrigerate until cool.
2. Accelerate to ice cream maker for freezing.

Nutrition:

- Calories: 165
- Protein: 138 g
- Carbs: 23 g
- Fat: 10 g
- Sugar: 8g

Lime Sorbet

Preparation Time: 1 hour and 45 minutes

Cooking Time: 1 hour

Servings: 6-8

Ingredients:

- 2 cups of water
- 3/4 cup freshly squeezed lime juice

Directions:

1. Place the sugar and 1 cup of the water in a small pot, and stream until all of the sugar is dissolved. Allow cooling to combine with the lime juice and the remaining 1 cup of water. Refrigerate until cool.
2. Accelerate to ice cream maker for freezing.

Nutrition:

- Calories: 112
- Protein: 118 g
- Carbs: 16 g
- Fat: 18 g
- Sugar: 8 g

Mango Sorbet

Preparation Time: 1 hour and 45 minutes

Cooking Time: 1 hour

Servings: 6-8

Ingredients:

- 3/4 cup of sugar
- 2/3 cup of water
- 2 tablespoons lime juice
- 2 pounds fresh mangos
- 1 teaspoon vanilla extract

Directions:

1. Set the sugar and water in a saucepan, and stream all of the sugar is dissolved. Combine with the lime juice.
2. Peel and chop the mangos. Stream the mangos in a food processor until smooth. Combine with the chilled syrup and vanilla.
3. Attach to ice cream maker for freezing.

Nutrition:

- Calories: 112
- Protein: 118 g

- Carbs: 16 g
- Fat: 18 g
- Sugar: 8 g

Lemonade Sorbet

Preparation Time: 1 hour

Cooking Time: 1 hour

Servings: 6-8

Ingredients:

- 1 cup of sugar
- 1 cup of water
- 1 cup prepared lemonade
- 3/4 cup freshly squeezed lemon juice

Directions:

1. Set the sugar and water in a small saucepan, and stir over medium heat until all of the sugar is dissolved. Allow cooling combine with the lemonade and lemon juice. Refrigerate until cool.
2. Accelerate to ice cream maker for freezing.

Nutrition:

- Calories: 132
- Protein: 128 g
- Carbs: 16 g
- Fat: 18 g

- Sugar: 8 g

Sparkling White Grape Sorbet

Preparation Time: 1 hour and 45 minutes

Cooking Time: 1 hour

Servings: 6-8

Ingredients:

- 4 pounds white grapes
- 1/4 cup of water
- 1/4 cup corn syrup
- 1/4 cup sparkling white grape juice

Directions:

1. Combine the grapes with the water in a large pot over medium heat.
2. Whip and cook the grapes until soft and liquidized. Detach from heat.
3. Squeeze the grapes through a mesh strainer to remove the seeds and skins.
4. Attach the corn syrup and sparkling juice to the grape mixture, and chill in the refrigerator until cool.
5. Attach to ice cream maker for freezing.

Nutrition:

- Calories: 112
- Protein: 184 g
- Carbs: 12 g
- Fat: 15 g
- Sugar: 18 g

Ginger Pear Sorbet

Preparation Time: 1 hour and 30 minutes

Cooking Time: 1 hour

Servings: 6

Ingredients:

- 3 pounds ripe pears
- 1 cup of water
- 1/4 teaspoon dried ginger
- 1 tablespoon lemon juice
- 3/4 cup of sugar

Directions:

1. Wash, core, and cut the pears; set with 1/2 cup of the water and the ginger in a medium-sized covered saucepan. Heat over medium heat, stirring occasionally, for 15–20 minutes, or until very tender.
2. Detach pears from heat and Combine the remaining water, lemon juice, and sugar in a blender, and process until smooth. Refrigerate until chilled.
3. Attach to ice cream maker for freezing.

Nutrition:

- Calories: 132
- Protein: 128 g
- Carbs: 16 g
- Fat: 18 g
- Sugar: 8 g

Watermelon Sorbet

Preparation Time: 1 hour and 30 minutes

Cooking Time: 1 hour

Servings: 6

Ingredients:

- 3 cups watermelon juice
- 2/3 cup of sugar
- 1/4 teaspoon salt
- 1 tablespoon freshly squeezed lemon juice
- 1/4 cup mini chocolate chips for "seeds"

Directions:

1. Remove the watermelon flesh from the rind, taking care to discard seeds. Purée in a food processor or blender until smooth to make 3 cups of watermelon juice.
2. Mix the sugar, salt, and 1 cup of watermelon juice in a saucepan and whip. Allow cooling to mix with the lemon juice and remaining watermelon juice.
3. Attach to ice cream maker for freezing. Add in chocolate chips toward the end of freezing.

Nutrition:

- Calories: 115
- Protein: 118 g
- Carbs: 28 g
- Fat: 18 g
- Sugar: 8 g

Cantaloupe Sorbet

Preparation Time: 1 hour and 30 minutes

Cooking Time: 1 hour

Servings: 6

Ingredients:

- 1 large, ripe cantaloupe
- 2/3 cup of sugar
- 1/4 teaspoon salt
- 1 teaspoon freshly squeezed lemon juice

Directions:

1. Detach the flesh from the rind of the cantaloupe, taking care to discard seeds and any green flesh. Purée in a food processor or blender until smooth.
2. Add the remaining ingredients and purée until well combined.
3. Attach to ice cream maker for freezing.

Nutrition:

- Calories: 185
- Protein: 116 g
- Carbs: 24 g
- Fat: 13 g
- Sugar: 10 g

Honeydew Sorbet

Preparation Time: 1 hour and 30 minutes

Cooking Time: 1 hour

Servings: 6

Ingredients:

- 1 large, ripe honeydew
- 1/2 cup of sugar
- Pinch salt
- 1 teaspoon freshly squeezed lime juice

Directions:

1. Detach the flesh from the rind of the melon, taking care to discard seeds and any unripe flesh. Purée in a food processor or blender until smooth.
2. Attach the remaining ingredients, and purée until well combined. Cover and refrigerate until cool.
3. Attach to ice cream maker for freezing.

Nutrition:

- Calories: 135
- Protein: 115 g
- Carbs: 23 g
- Fat: 19 g
- Sugar: 11 g

Bing cherry Sorbet

Preparation Time: 1 hour and 40 minutes

Cooking Time: 2 hours

Servings: 4-6

Ingredients:

- 21/2 pounds Bing cherries
- 3/4 cup of water
- 1 cup of sugar
- 2 teaspoons lemon juice
- 1/2 teaspoon vanilla extract

Directions:

1. Clean the cherries, and mix with the water, sugar, and lemon juice in a saucepan
2. Whip and cook the cherries until soft and liquidized.
3. Detach from heat, and cool to room temperature.
4. Bring cherries and vanilla in blender and purée until smooth. Refrigerate until thoroughly chilled.
5. Attach to ice cream maker for freezing.

Nutrition:

- Calories: 115
- Protein: 110 g
- Carbs: 20 g
- Fat: 18 g
- Sugar: 12 g

Popsicles

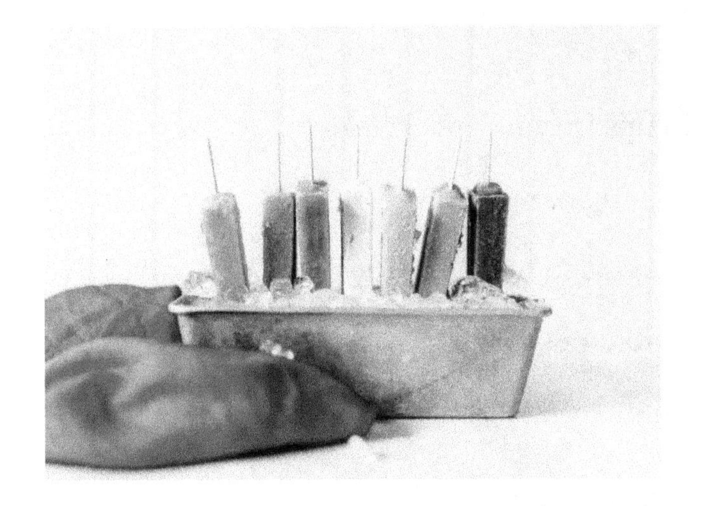

Dark Cherry Chocolate Popsicles

Preparation Time: 30 minutes

Cooking Time: 1 hour

Servings: 4-6

Ingredients:

- 2 cups frozen dark cherries
- 1/2 cup of milk
- 1 teaspoon vanilla extract
- 2 tablespoons maple extract
- 4 oz. chocolate, melted

Directions:

1. Put the dark cherries, milk, vanilla, and maple extract in a blender and pulse until smooth.
2. Mix the melted chocolate and pulse a few more times until well blended.
3. Stream the mixture into your Popsicle molds and freeze for at least 3 hours or even better, overnight.

Nutrition:

- Calories: 150
- Protein: 110 g
- Carbs: 30 g
- Fat: 58 g
- Sugar: .9.7 g

Lemon and Lime Popsicles

Preparation Time: 30 minutes

Cooking Time: 1 hour

Servings: 4-6

Ingredients:

- 2 lemons juice
- 2 limes juice
- 1/2 cup of sugar
- 1/2 cup of water
- 1 lime and 1/2 lemon zest

Directions:

1. Pour the water into a small saucepan.
2. Stir in the sugar and zest and bring to a boil.
3. Remove from heat and let it infuse for 10 minutes then strain.
4. Stream in the lime and lemon juice and pour the mixture into Popsicle molds.
5. Freeze for at least 3 hours or overnight.

Nutrition:

- Calories: 150
- Protein: 110 g
- Carbs: 30 g
- Fat: 58 g
- Sugar: .9.7 g

Lemon Cream Popsicles

Preparation Time: 30 minutes

Cooking Time: 1 hour

Servings: 8

Ingredients:

- 2 cups plain yogurt
- 1/2 cup of water
- 1/2 cup of sugar
- 1 teaspoon vanilla extract
- 1 tablespoon fresh lemon zest
- 2 tablespoons lemon juice

Directions:

1. Mix the water and sugar in a small saucepan and bring to a boil.
2. Simmer for 5 minutes.
3. Remove from heat and stir in the lemon zest.
4. Let it cool.
5. Add the yogurt, vanilla, and lemon juice.
6. Stream this mixture into your Popsicle molds and freeze for 4 hours or more.

Nutrition:

- Calories: 140
- Protein: 210 g
- Carbs: 38 g
- Fat: 18 g
- Sugar: .10 g

Passion Fruit and White Chocolate Popsicles

Preparation Time: 30 minutes

Cooking Time: 1 hour

Servings: 6

Ingredients:

- 3 passion fruits
- 2/3 cup of milk
- 1/2 cup heavy cream
- 1/4 cup of sugar
- 2 egg yolks
- 5oz white chocolate

Directions:

1. Slice all the passion fruits in half and scoop the flesh into a sieve.
2. Press it through the sieve and discard the seeds.
3. Transfer into a bowl and put aside.
4. Pour the milk and cream into a saucepan and bring it to the boiling point. In the meantime, in another bowl, mix

the egg yolks with the sugar until pale then gradually pour in the hot milk.

5. Transfer back into the saucepan and put it on low heat.
6. Cook until it starts to thicken then remove from heat and while still hot, stir in the white chocolate.
7. Mix well until melted.
8. When cold, mix in the passion fruit and pour the mixture into Popsicle molds.
9. Freeze at least 5 hours before serving.

Nutrition:

- Calories: 140
- Protein: 210 g
- Carbs: 38 g
- Fat: 18 g
- Sugar: .10 g

Strawberry Cheesecake Popsicles

Preparation Time: 30 minutes

Cooking Time: 1 hour

Servings: 8

Ingredients:

- 10 oz. cream cheese
- 2/3 cup heavy cream
- 1/2 cup of milk
- 1/3 cup of sugar
- 1 teaspoon vanilla extract
- 2 cups fresh strawberries

Directions:

1. Divide the strawberries into 2 parts. Chop 1 cup of them and put them aside then puree the other half.
2. Mix the cream cheese with the heavy cream, milk, and sugar.
3. Stir in the vanilla and strawberry puree then fold in the chopped strawberries.
4. Pour the mixture evenly into Popsicle molds and freeze at least 4 hours before serving.

Nutrition:

- Calories: 240
- Protein: 290 g
- Carbs: 38 g
- Fat: 10 g
- Sugar: .10 g

Peanut Butter and Chocolate Popsicles

Preparation Time: 30 minutes

Cooking Time: 1 hour

Servings: 6-8

Ingredients:

- 1 cup cream cheese
- 1 cup heavy cream
- 1 cup peanut butter
- 1/2 cup chocolate chips
- 1/4 cup of sugar
- 1 teaspoon vanilla extract

Directions:

1. Mix the cream cheese with the sugar well then adds the heavy cream, peanut butter, and vanilla.
2. Set in the chocolate chips and pour the mixture into your Popsicle molds.
3. Freeze for at least 4 hours.
4. Just before serving sink the molds into hot water for 5 seconds then take them out.

Nutrition:

- Calories: 240
- Protein: 290 g
- Carbs: 38 g
- Fat: 10 g
- Sugar: .10 g

Raspberry Cheesecake Popsicle

Preparation Time: 30 minutes

Cooking Time: 1 hour

Servings: 6-8

Ingredients:

- 2 cups raspberries
- 1 cup heavy cream
- 1 cup cream cheese
- 1 teaspoon vanilla extract
- 4 tablespoons honey

Directions:

1. Mix the cream cheese with the heavy cream and vanilla.
2. Add the honey to taste then fold in the raspberries.
3. Set the mixture into Popsicle molds.
4. Freeze at least for 3 hours before serving.
5. To take them out of their molds sunk them in hot water for a few seconds.

Nutrition:

- Calories: 240
- Protein: 290 g
- Carbs: 38 g
- Fat: 10 g
- Sugar: .10 g

Caramelized Pear and Ginger Popsicles

Preparation Time: 30 minutes

Cooking Time: 1 hour

Servings: 6-8

Ingredients:

- 1 pound pears, peeled, cored, and diced
- 1/4 cup butter
- 1/2 cup brown sugar
- 2 tablespoons lemon juice
- 1 teaspoon vanilla extract
- 1 tablespoon chopped ginger

Directions:

1. Dissolve the butter in a large heavy skillet and add the ginger.
2. Cook for 2-3 minutes until fragrant.
3. Stir in the brown sugar and cook for a few more minutes until it starts to melt.
4. Add the lemon juice and pears and cook those 5-10 minutes until soft.
5. Remove from heat and let it cool.

6. When chilled, pour into a blender, add the vanilla, and pulse until smooth.
7. Pour into your Popsicle molds and freeze at least 4 hours before serving.

Nutrition:

- Calories: 340
- Protein: 290 g
- Carbs: 78 g
- Fat: 18 g
- Sugar: .10 g

Apple Cider Popsicles

Preparation Time: 15 minutes

Cooking Time: 45 minutes

Servings: 6-8

Ingredients:

- 4 cups apple juice
- 1/2 cup of sugar
- 1/2 cup of water
- 1 teaspoon cinnamon
- 2 whole cloves
- 2 tablespoons apple cider vinegar
- 1 teaspoon vanilla extract

Directions:

1. Mix the apple juice, sugar, water, cinnamon, cloves, and bring to a boil.
2. Set on low heat for 30 minutes until the liquid has significantly reduced.
3. Remove from heat and let it cool to room temperature
4. Stir in the cider and vanilla.
5. Strain and pour into your Popsicle molds.

6. Freeze at least 4 hours before serving.

Nutrition:

- Calories: 340
- Protein: 290 g
- Carbs: 78 g
- Fat: 18 g
- Sugar: .10 g

Coconut Chocolate Popsicles

Preparation Time: 15 minutes

Cooking Time: 45 minutes

Servings: 6-8

Ingredients:

- 1 1/2 cups coconut milk
- 1/3 cup of sugar
- 1/2 cup heavy cream
- 1/4 cup desiccated coconut
- 1/2 cup chocolate chips
- 1 teaspoon vanilla extract

Directions:

1. Mix the coconut milk with sugar, heavy cream, and desiccated coconut
2. Add the vanilla and chocolate chips.
3. Stream this mixture into your Popsicle molds.
4. Freeze at least 3 hours before serving. Enjoy!

Nutrition:

- Calories: 240
- Protein: 270 g
- Carbs: 77 g
- Fat: 23 g
- Sugar: .19 g

Cake and Pies

All-American Banana Split

Preparation Time: 5 minutes

Cooking Time: 1 hour

Servings: 4-6

Ingredients:

- 1 medium banana
- 1 scoop vanilla, chocolate, and strawberry
- 2 tbsp. sliced fresh strawberries or 1 tbsp. strawberry ice cream topping
- 2 tbsp. pineapple chunks or 1 tbsp. pineapple ice cream topping
- 2 tbsp. whipped cream
- 1 tbsp. chopped peanuts
- 1 tbsp. chocolate syrup
- 2 maraschino cherries with stems

Directions:

1. In a dessert dish, place banana.
2. Arrange scoops of ice cream among banana.
3. Place the rest of the ingredients atop.
4. Serve right away.

Nutrition:

- Calories: 346
- Protein: 240 g
- Carbs: 79 g
- Fat: 23.8 g
- Sugar: .15 g

Blueberry Shortcake Sundaes

Preparation Time: 5 minutes

Cooking Time: 1 hour

Servings: 4-6

Ingredients:

- 2 cups heavy whipping cream
- 1 cup half-and-half
- 3/4 cup white sugar
- 5 tbsp. amaretto liqueur (such as Disaronno)
- 1 tsp. vanilla extract

Directions:

1. In a big bowl, combine sugar, half-and-half, and heavy cream until the sugar dissolves.
2. Add vanilla extract and amaretto liqueur.
3. Add the milk mixture to an ice cream maker and freeze following the manufacturer's directions until the ice cream has a 'soft-serve' consistency.
4. Remove the ice cream to a container with a lid.
5. Freeze for approximately 2 hours before enjoying.

Nutrition:

- Calories: 237 calories
- Total Carbohydrate: 17.6 g
- Cholesterol: 62 mg
- Total Fat: 17 g
- Protein: 1.4 g
- Sodium: 24 mg
- Sugar: 21 g

Apple Caramel Ice Cream

Preparation Time: 51 minutes

Cooking Time: 1 hour and 30 minutes

Servings: 16

Ingredients:

- 2 cups heavy whipping cream
- 1 can sweeten condensed milk
- 1/2 cup applesauce
- 1/4 cup caramel sauce
- 3 tbsp. salted butter, melted
- 1/2 tsp. vanilla extract
- 1/2 tsp. salt

Directions:

1. Stream the cream until it forms stiff peaks.
2. When you lift the whisk or beater straight up, sharp peaks should be formed from the cream.
3. Whisk in salt, vanilla extract, butter, caramel sauce, applesauce, and sweetened condensed milk until thoroughly incorporated.

4. Transfer the cream mixture to a large container and cover it.
5. Place in freezer for about 6 hours until hard.

Nutrition:

- Calories: 217 calories
- Total Carbohydrate: 18.4 g
- Cholesterol: 55 mg
- Total Fat: 15.3 g
- Protein: 2.7 g
- Sodium: 148 mg
- Sugar: 11 g

Brownie Chunk Ice-Cream

Preparation Time: 5 minutes

Cooking Time: 45 minutes

Servings: 8

Ingredients:

- 8 oatmeal cookies, crushed
- 2 tbsp. melted butter, divided
- 2 large apples, peeled, cored, and sliced
- 3 tbsp. white sugar
- 1 tsp. ground cinnamon
- 3 cups whipping cream
- 1 1/2 cups half and half
- 1 cup white sugar
- 3 eggs, beaten
- 1 tsp. vanilla extract
- 2 tsp. ground cinnamon
- 1/4 cup walnuts
- 1/4 cup caramel ice cream topping

Directions:

1. Start preheating the oven to 375 °F (190 °C.)
2. Mix one tbsp. melted butter with crushed cookies, then press onto the baking sheet. Bake for 5 mines in the prepared oven. Then take out, let cool completely. Crumble.
3. In a skillet, melt the remaining one tbsp. butter over medium heat. Mix in one tsp. of cinnamon, 3 tbsp. of sugar and apples. Cook for 10 mins. or until the sugar has started to caramelize and apples have browned lightly. Take away from the pan, let cool completely.
4. In a large bowl, combine 2 tsp. of cinnamon, vanilla, eggs, one cup of the sugar, half and half, and cream; blend well by mixing. Transfer to the ice cream maker; freeze following the manufacturer's directions.
5. Stir in walnuts, caramelized apples, and crumbled cookies once the ice cream has been done. Put in dulcet de lecher by tsp., stirring to distribute evenly.

Nutrition:

- Calories: 780 Total Carbohydrate: 63.9 g
- Cholesterol: 233 mg Total Fat: 56 g
- Protein: 9.8 g Sodium: 270 mg

- Sugar: 13 g

Baked Alaska

Preparation Time: 20 minutes

Cooking Time: 5 hours

Servings: 16

Ingredients:

- 2 quarts vanilla ice cream, softened
- 1 (18.25 oz.) package white cake mix
- 1 egg
- 1/2 tsp. almond extract
- 8 egg whites
- 1/8 tsp. cream of tartar
- 1/8 tsp. salt
- 1 cup white sugar

Directions:

1. Use foil to line a deep 8″ square container or 8″ round mixing bowl, both bottom and sides. Fill the container with ice cream; pack tightly. Freeze with a cover for 8 hours or until set.
2. Set oven to 175 °C (or 350 °F) and start preheating. Butter and dust an 8x8″ pan with flour.

3. Combine cake mix with almond extract and egg pour into the greased pan.
4. Bake in the prepared oven following directions on the package until the cake is springy to the touch of a hand.
5. Whisk sugar, salt, cream of tartar with egg whites until it forms firm peaks.
6. Use heavy brown paper or parchment to line a baking sheet. Arrange the cake in the middle of the sheet. Turn molded ice cream on top of the cake. Spread meringue nicely and quickly, all over the cake, ice cream, and all the way to the lined paper to enclose. Leave in the freezer for 2 hours.
7. Start preheating the oven to 220 °C (or 425 ° F).
8. Place Alaska on the lowest shelf in the oven and bake for 8-10 minutes, or until meringue turns brown a little. Serve immediately.

Nutrition:

- Calories: 330
- Total Carbohydrate: 53.1 g
- Cholesterol: 41 mg
- Total Fat: 11.1 g
- Protein: 6 g
- Sodium: 315 mg
- Sugar: 12 g

Banana and Peanut Butter 4-Ingredient 'Ice Cream'

Preparation Time: 10 minutes

Cooking Time: 2 hours

Servings: 8

Ingredients:

- 2 slightly overripe bananas cut into chunks
- 1 tsp. confectioners' sugar (optional)
- 1/2 tsp. milk
- 2 drops vanilla extract
- 1 tsp. peanut butter, or more to taste

Directions:

1. On a plate, place banana chunks; freeze for 2 hours until solid.
2. In a blender, put vanilla extract, milk, confectioners' sugar, and frozen bananas; blend until creamy and smooth.
3. Add in peanut butter, process until smooth.

Nutrition:

- Calories: 129
- Total Carbohydrate: 28.9 g
- Cholesterol: 51 mg
- Total Fat: 1.8 g
- Protein: 2 g
- Sodium: 14 mg
- Sugar: 11 g

Banana Citrus Sorbet

Preparation Time: 15 minutes

Cooking Time: 45 minutes

Servings: 2 1/2 quarts

Ingredients:

- 1/2 cup lemon juice
- 3 medium ripe bananas cut into chunks
- 1-1/2 cups sugar
- 2 cups cold water
- 1-1/2 cups orange juice

Directions:

1. Combine bananas and lemon juice in a blender.
2. Put the cover on and process until smooth.
3. Mix in sugar and process, while covered, until incorporated.
4. Pour mixture into a big bowl and pour in orange juice and water.
5. Fill ice cream freezer cylinder two-thirds.
6. Freeze the sorbet according to the manufacturer's instructions.

7. Pour the sorbet into a freezer canister, leave a bit of space to allow the mixture to expand.
8. Keep in the freezer for 2 to 4 hours, and then serve.
9. Follow the same steps when working with the rest of the sorbet mixture.

Nutrition:

- Calories: 168
- Total Carbohydrate: 43 g
- Cholesterol: 0 mg
- Total Fat: 0 g
- Fiber: 1 g
- Protein: 1 g
- Sodium: 1 mg
- Sugar: 12 g

Banana Rum Sundaes for Two

Preparation Time: 10 minutes

Cooking Time: 20 minutes

Servings: 2

Ingredients:

- 1 tbsp. butter
- 1/4 cup packed brown sugar
- Dash ground nutmeg
- 2 medium firm bananas, halved and sliced
- 2 tbsp. golden raisins
- 1 tbsp. rum
- 1 tbsp. sliced almonds, toasted
- 1-1/3 cups vanilla ice cream

Directions:

1. Dissolve the butter in a large nonstick skillet on medium-low heat.
2. Stir brown sugar and nutmeg into the mix till blended.
3. Turn off heat; add the almonds, raisins, rum, and bananas.

4. Cook on medium heat, stirring gently until bananas are slightly softened and glazed for about 3-4 minutes.
5. Serve alongside the ice cream.

Nutrition:

- Calories: 497
- Total Carbohydrate: 82 g
- Cholesterol: 54 mg
- Total Fat: 17 g
- Fiber: 4 g
- Protein: 5 g
- Sodium: 124 mg
- Sugar: 5 g

Banana Split Cheesecake

Preparation Time: 5 minutes

Cooking Time: 45 minutes

Servings: 18

Ingredients:

- 2 1/2 cups graham cracker crumbs
- 3/4 cup melted butter
- 4 cups confectioners' sugar
- 2 (8 oz.) packages cream cheese
- 1 (8 oz.) can crushed pineapple, drained
- 3 medium bananas, quartered
- 1 container frozen whipped,
- 8 maraschino cherries, halved
- 1/4 cup chocolate syrup
- 1/2 cup pecan halves

Directions:

1. Combine melted margarine or butter with graham crackers; press mixture into the bottom of a 9x12-inch pan.

2. Beat cream cheese with confectioners' sugar until smooth.
3. Spread over graham cracker layer.
4. Arrange bananas and crushed pineapple over the cream cheese.
5. Top with a spreading layer of whipped topping.
6. Garnish on top with maraschino cherry halves.
7. Drizzle over the top with chocolate syrup and scatter with pecans.
8. Refrigerate for a minimum of 4 hours before serving.

Nutrition:

- Calories: 428
- Total Carbohydrate: 50.9 g
- Cholesterol: 48 mg
- Total Fat: 24.6 g
- Protein: 3.6 g
- Sodium: 207 mg
- Sugar: 3 g

Banana Split Dessert

Preparation Time: 5 minutes

Cooking Time: 45 minutes

Servings: 8

Ingredients:

- 1/2 cups crushed graham cracker crumbs
- 3 tablespoons butter, melted
- 3 bananas, sliced
- 1 can crushed pineapple, drained
- 1 1/2 cups blueberries, fresh
- 1 1/2 cups strawberries, halved; if using frozen, thaw and drain
- 1 pint light whipping cream
- 3 tablespoons sugar

Directions:

1. Mix graham cracker crumbs and melted butter.
2. Batter the cream until it forms stiff peaks. Whip in sugar. Chill while you prepare the fruit.
3. Strain the pineapple. Peel and cut the bananas. Clean the blueberries. Wash and clean the strawberries; slice in

half. You can use frozen berries, but make sure to defrost them completely and strain.

4. Assemble the dessert.
5. Put half of the whipping cream over the graham cracker shell evenly. Layer bananas over, then put strained pineapple on top; garnish with blueberries and strawberries. Spread leftover whipping cream on top.
6. Chill for a few hours. Enjoy!

Nutrition:

- Calories: 346
- Protein: 240 g
- Carbs: 79 g
- Fat: 23.8 g
- Sugar: .15 g

Healthy Desserts

Vegan Chocolate Soft Serve Ice-Cream

Preparation Time: 50 minutes

Cooking Time: 10 minutes

Servings: 9

Ingredients:

- 3/4 cup of water
- 1 1/4 cups coconut milk
- 2/3 cup organic cane sugar
- 2/3 cup unsweetened cocoa powder
- 1/4 tsp. sea salt
- 6 ounces vegan dark chocolate, finely chopped
- 1/2 tsp. pure vanilla extract

Directions:

1. Mix the first 5 ingredients: and heat it on medium-high heat. Mix the ingredients together using a whisk. Let come to a low boil. Pursue to whisk often, and remain cooking on a low boil for 1 minute.
2. Bring the pan off the heat, and mix in the chocolate and vanilla extract using the whisk.

3. Allow the mixture to cool
4. Pour the ingredients into the canister, follow the instructions above to set up your ice cream maker.
5. Serve immediately.

Nutrition:

- Calories: 130
- Protein: 110.7 g
- Carbs: 29.9 g
- Fat: 18 g
- Sugar: .9.7 g

Vegan Radical Raspberry Chocolate Ice-Cream

Preparation Time: 50 minutes

Cooking Time: 10 minutes

Servings: 9

Ingredients:

- 3/4 cup of water
- 1 1/4 cups coconut milk
- 2/3 cup organic cane sugar
- 2/3 cup unsweetened cocoa powder
- 1/4 tsp. sea salt
- 6 ounces vegan dark chocolate, finely chopped
- 1/2 tsp. pure vanilla extract
- 1/2 cup raspberries

Directions:

1. Mix the first 5 ingredients in a large saucepan, and heat it on medium-high heat. Mix the ingredients together using a whisk.
2. Bring the pan off the heat, and mix in the chocolate and vanilla extract using the whisk

3. Bring the mixture in a blender with the raspberries, and blend on high speed for about 30 seconds or until the raspberries are pureed.
4. Allow the mixture to cool
5. Pour the ingredients into the canister, follow the instructions above to set up your ice cream maker.
6. Serve immediately.

Nutrition:

- Calories: 150
- Protein: 112 g
- Carbs: 20 g
- Fat: 25 g
- Sugar: 10 g

Vegan “Oh So” Soy Vanilla Ice-Cream

Preparation Time: 50 minutes

Cooking Time: 10 minutes

Servings: 9

Ingredients:

- 1 pound silken tofu
- 1/2 cup plus 2 tablespoons organic or granulated sugar
- 1/2 teaspoon kosher salt
- 1 vanilla bean, split lengthwise
- 3/4 cup refined coconut oil, melted, cooled slightly

Directions:

1. Put the first 3 ingredients in a blender. Then add in the vanilla bean seeds. Puree the mixture until smooth, around 15 seconds. Blend the mixture until its thick, but don’t over blend it.
2. Pour the ingredients into the canister; follow the instructions above to set up your ice cream maker.
3. Serve immediately.

Nutrition:

- Calories: 150
- Protein: 112 g
- Carbs: 20 g
- Fat: 25 g
- Sugar: 10 g

Vegan Chunky Chocolate Almond Ice-Cream

Preparation Time: 15 minutes

Cooking Time: 10 minutes

Servings: 9

Ingredients:

- 3/4 cup of water
- 1 1/4 cups coconut milk
- 2/3 cup organic cane sugar
- 2/3 cup unsweetened cocoa powder
- 1/4 tsp. sea salt
- 6 ounces vegan dark chocolate, finely chopped
- 1/2 tsp. pure vanilla extract
- 1/2 cup chopped almonds

Directions:

1. Mix the first 5 ingredients, and heat it on medium-high heat. Mix the ingredients together using a whisk. Continue to whisk often, and remain cooking on a low boil for 1 minute.

2. Bring the pan off the heat, and mix in the chocolate and vanilla extract using the whisk. Whisk until the chocolate is melted.
3. Bring the mixture and blend at high speed for about 30 seconds.
4. Allow the mixture to cool
5. Pour all the ingredients into the canister and stir well, follow the instructions above to set up your ice cream maker.
6. Bring the ice cream in an airtight container and place it in the freezer for around 2 hours. Let the ice cream to thaw before serving.

Nutrition:

- Calories: 170
- Protein: 182 g
- Carbs: 28 g
- Fat: 35 g
- Sugar: 15 g

Vegan Sensuous Strawberries N Cream Ice-Cream

Preparation Time: 35 minutes

Cooking Time: 10 minutes

Servings: 1 quart

Ingredients:

- 1 pound tofu
- 1/2 cup plus 2 tablespoons organic
- 1/2 teaspoon kosher salt
- 1 vanilla bean, split lengthwise
- 3/4 cup refined coconut oil, melted, cooled slightly
- 1 cup sliced strawberries

Directions:

1. Mix the first 3 ingredients in a blender. Then add in the vanilla bean seeds and strawberries. Puree the mixture until smooth, around 15 seconds. Blend the mixture until its thick, but don't over blend it.
2. Pour all the ingredients into the canister and stir well, follow the instructions above to set up your ice cream maker.

3. Bring the ice cream in an airtight container and place in the freezer for around 2 hours.

Nutrition:

- Calories: 270
- Protein: 192 g
- Carbs: 58 g
- Fat: 30 g
- Sugar: 10 g

Vegan Soy Vanilla and Carob Chip Ice-Cream

Preparation Time: 35 minutes

Cooking Time: 45 minutes

Servings: 1 quart

Ingredients:

- 1 pound tofu
- 1/2 cup granulated sugar
- 1/2 teaspoon kosher salt
- 1 vanilla bean, split lengthwise
- 3/4 cup refined coconut oil, melted, cooled slightly
- 1 cup vegan carob chips

Directions:

1. Mix the first 3 ingredients in a blender. Then add in the vanilla bean seeds. Puree the mixture until smooth, around 15 seconds. Turn the blender to medium speed, and slowly drizzle in the coconut oil. Blend the mixture until its thick, but don't over blend it.

2. Pour all the ingredients into the canister and stir well, follow the instructions above to set up your ice cream maker.
3. Put the ice cream in a container and place in the freezer for around 2 hours.
4. Bring the ice cream to freeze for 15 minutes before serving.

Nutrition:

- Calories: 170
- Protein: 122 g
- Carbs: 59 g
- Fat: 37 g
- Sugar: 12 g

Vegan Pistachio "Punch" Chocolate Chunk Gelato

Preparation Time: 2 hours 35 minutes

Cooking Time: 45 minutes

Servings: 4

Ingredients:

- 2 cups shelled, roasted, salted pistachios
- 1 can coconut milk
- 1/2 cup arrowroot
- 3/4 cup of sugar
- 1 teaspoon lime juice
- 4 ounces chopped vegan chocolate

Directions:

1. Place the pistachios in a food processor for about 3 minutes
2. Place all ingredients except the chocolate in a blender. Blend on high speed until smooth.
3. Pour all the ingredients into the canister and stir well, follow the instructions above to set up your ice cream maker.

4. Put the gelato in an airtight container and place in the freezer for up to 2 hours, until the desired consistency is reached.

Nutrition:

- Calories: 170
- Protein: 122 g
- Carbs: 59 g
- Fat: 37 g
- Sugar: 12 g

Vegan Sweet Chocolate Strawberry Chunk Gelato

Preparation Time: 2 hours 35 minutes

Cooking Time: 45 minutes

Servings: 4

Ingredients:

- 1 cup refrigerated coconut cream
- 1 cup pitted dates
- 1 cup of frozen banana pieces
- 3 tablespoons cocoa powder
- 1/2 teaspoon salt
- 1/2 cup strawberry cut into chunk

Directions:

1. Mix all ingredients except the strawberries in a blender. Blend on high speed until smooth.
2. Pour all the ingredients into the canister and stir well, follow the instructions above to set up your ice cream maker.

3. Put the gelato in an airtight container and place in the freezer for up to 2 hours, until the desired consistency is reached.

Nutrition:

- Calories: 156
- Protein: 126 g
- Carbs: 56 g
- Fat: 36 g
- Sugar: 16 g

Vegan Big Blackberry Soy Frozen Yogurt

Preparation Time: 2 hours 35 minutes

Cooking Time: 45 minutes

Servings: 1 quart

Ingredients:

- 2 3/4 cups unsweetened plain soy yogurt
- 11/4 blackberry jam

Directions:

1. Mix the yogurt into a bowl and combine it with the jam. Use a hand mixer to beat the mixture for 5 minutes.
2. Pour the ingredients into the canister, follow the instructions above to set up your ice cream maker.
3. Put the frozen yogurt in an airtight container and place in the freezer for at least 2 hours, until the desired consistency is reached.

Nutrition:

- Calories: 256
- Protein: 122 g
- Carbs: 156 g
- Fat: 136 g
- Sugar: 16 g

Vegan Ridiculous Raspberry Coconut Frozen Yogurt

Preparation Time: 2 hours 35 minutes

Cooking Time: 45 minutes

Servings: 1 quart

Ingredients:

- 2 cups of coconut yogurt
- 1/4 cup of sugar or maple syrup
- 1/2 teaspoon vanilla extract
- 1/4 cup shredded coconut
- 1/2 cup raspberries

Directions:

1. Mix the raspberries in a blender.
2. Place the yogurt in a bowl. Continue to whisk for about 4 minutes until the sugar dissolves. Then mix in the vanilla extract, and raspberry puree.
3. Pour all the ingredients into the canister and stir well, follow the instructions above to set up your ice cream maker.

4. Put the frozen yogurt in an airtight container and place in the freezer for at least 2 hours, until the desired consistency is reached.

Nutrition:

- Calories: 156
- Protein: 162 g
- Carbs: 116 g
- Fat: 16 g
- Sugar: 18 g

Standard U.S./ Metric Measurement Conversions

Volume Conversions

U.S. Volume Measure	**Metric Equivalent**
1/8 teaspoon	0.5 milliliters
1/4 teaspoon	1 milliliter
1/2 teaspoon	2 milliliters
1 teaspoon	5 milliliters
1/2 tablespoon	7 milliliters
1 tablespoon (3 teaspoons)	15 milliliters
2 tablespoons (1 fluid ounce)	30 milliliters

1/4 cup (4 tablespoons)	60 milliliters
1/3 cup	90 milliliters
1/2 cup (4 fluid ounces)	125 milliliters
2/3 cup	160 milliliters
3/4 cup (6 fluid ounces)	180 milliliters
1 cup (16 tablespoons)	250 milliliters
1 pint (2 cups)	500 milliliters
1 quart (4 cups)	1 liter (about)
Weight Conversions	
U.S. Weight Measure	**Metric Equivalent**
1/2 ounce	15 grams
1 ounce	30 grams
2 ounces	60 grams
3 ounces	85 grams
1/4 pound (4 ounces)	115 grams
1/2 pound (8 ounces)	225 grams
3/4 pound (12 ounces)	340 grams
1 pound (16 ounces)	454 grams
Oven Temperature Conversions	

Degrees Fahrenheit	Degrees Celsius
200 degrees F	95 degrees C
250 degrees F	120 degrees C
275 degrees F	135 degrees C
300 degrees F	150 degrees C
325 degrees F	160 degrees C
350 degrees F	180 degrees C
375 degrees F	190 degrees C
400 degrees F	205 degrees C
425 degrees F	220 degrees C
450 degrees F	230 degrees C
Baking Pan Sizes	
American	**Metric**
8 × 11/2 inches round baking pan	20 × 4 cm cake tin
9 × 11/2 inches round baking pan	23 × 3.5 cm cake tin
11 × 7 × 11/2 inches baking pan	28 × 18 × 4 cm baking tin
13 × 9 × 2 inches baking pan	30 × 20 × 5 cm baking tin

2-quarts rectangular baking dish	30 × 20 × 3 cm baking tin
15 × 10 × 2 inches baking pan	30 × 25 × 2 cm baking tin (Swiss roll tin)
9-inches pie plate	22 × 4 or 23 × 4 cm pie plate
7 or 8-inches spring form pan	18 or 20 cm spring form or loose bottom cake tin
9 × 5 × 3 inches loaf pan	23 × 13 × 7 cm or 2 lb. narrow loaf or pate tin
11/2 quarts casserole	1.5-liters casserole
2-quarts casserole	2-liters casserole

Conclusion

Ice cream makers and food processors have a place in our kitchen, but sometimes the time just doesn't exist for multi-step, long process recipes. Get a Yonanas Healthy Dessert Maker and get instant dessert.

Its lightweight, the all-in-one-piece model, makes it super easy to store, clean, and travel with. Everything can be attached, which means no loose pieces will be falling all over the place when it's pulled out of storage or off the shelf. The important parts are all dishwasher safe, so only limited scrubbing is required. Make dessert and instantly enjoy it instead of spending time cleaning up and staring at the clock waiting for the moment it's finally frozen enough to eat.

Enjoy instant ice creams and sorbets, frozen cakes, pies and Popsicles, and even some non-dessert dishes like hummus and mashed potatoes.

With the market as saturated with blenders and ice cream makers, it can be hard to make a decision about which product to purchase. Educating yourself about other products and how they stack up against the Yonanas Healthy Dessert Maker is the best solution.

Perfect for making ice cream. This may seem obvious, but this is exactly what small appliances like the Cuisinart ICE-100 were created to do. Making your ice cream at home can be beneficial since you can control the ingredients. You can control dietary restrictions like dairy and opt for almond or coconut milk, and you can cut back on the amount of sugar that goes into your dessert. Some ice cream makers are 100% automatic and come with self-freezing bowls, yielding instant gratification with ready to eat ice cream. However, ice cream makers come at a cost. Most of these appliances pack quite a punch to your pocketbook and are incredibly difficult to clean and maintain. They contribute to weight loss. It turns out the limiting carbs in your desserts and emphasizing more on fats leads to more weight loss and improvement in overall health. The science behind this relates to the phenomenon of fuel for the body. For our body, the carb is a go-to source for energy. And when it gets digested, it is converted into glucose and then burned for fuel. So, if you consume carb-filled food and no other nutrients like fat and protein, the fat in your body lingers and adds on if you fail, you burn all the carb reserves in your body.

When you restrict carb in your diet, the body switches to a fat-burning mood and creates ketones, which is another source of energy that the body can use. When this happens, the body enters into a metabolic state called ketosis, which will result in the burning and reduction of stored fat in the body. Moreover, this process will keep you energetic without spiking your blood sugar levels.

It improves your overall health. Beyond the significant benefit of keno desserts, which is weight loss, another advantage is substantial improvement in general health. It is proved scientifically that many ailments reduce significantly after eating low-carb consistently, like high blood pressure, coronary diseases, diabetes, epilepsy, dementia, and cancer.

With all these benefits, you might just forget about desserts, but the good news is that you don't have to.

CPSIA information can be obtained
at www.ICGtesting.com
Printed in the USA
BVHW051710120521
607127BV00002B/335